THIS LAND CALLED AMERICA: TENNESSEE

CREATIVE EDUCATION

Published by Creative Education
P.O. Box 227, Mankato, Minnesota 56002
Creative Education is an imprint of The Creative Company
www.thecreativecompany.us

Design by Blue Design (www.bluedes.com)
Art direction by Rita Marshall
Book production by The Design Lab
Printed in the United States of America

Photographs by Alamy (Daniel Dempster Photography, Danita Delimont,
Lee Foster, H. Mark Weidman Photography, Andre Jenny, Bryon Jorjorian,
Michael Snell, Stock Connection Blue, Tom Till), Corbis (Bettmann, Blue
Lantern Studio, Kevin Fleming, Dave G. Houser, Minnesota Historical Society,
James Randklev), Getty Images (Altrendo Panoramic, Imagno, Michael Ochs
Archives, Paul Spinelli), iStockphoto (Karin Mortimer, Michael Thompson)

Library of Congress Cataloging-in-Publication Data
Gish, Melissa.
Tennessee / by Melissa Gish.
p. cm. — (This land called America)
Includes bibliographical references and index.
ISBN 978-1-58341-795-9
1. Tennessee—Juvenile literature. I. Title. II. Series.
F436.3.G57 2009
976.8—dc22   2008009524

First Edition
9 8 7 6 5 4 3 2 1

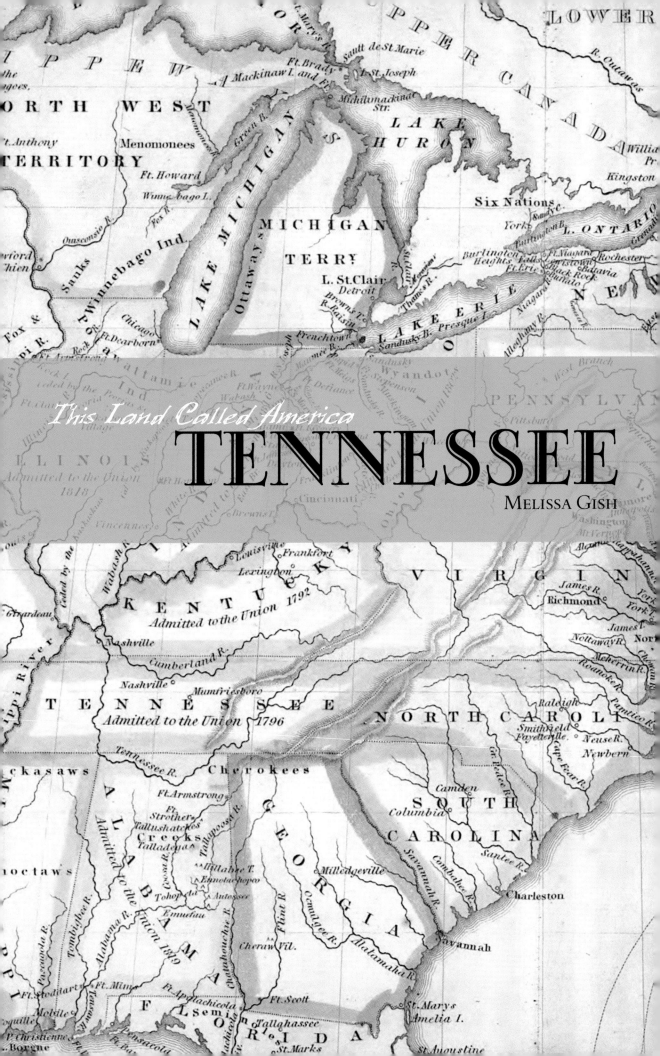

This Land Called America
TENNESSEE
Melissa Gish

Tennessee

MELISSA GISH

THE WARM MORNING SUN RISES OVER THE TOPS OF TALL PINE TREES ACROSS A GLASSY LAKE. A FISHERMAN WEARING RUBBER OVERALLS STANDS WAIST-DEEP IN THE WATER. WITH A PRECISE RHYTHM, HE BENDS HIS ELBOW, RAISING HIS FISHING ROD UPWARD AND THEN DROPPING IT BACK TO SHOULDER LEVEL. THE FISHING LINE MAKES A PERFECT ARC HIGH ABOVE THE MAN'S HEAD BEFORE THE END OF THE LINE DIPS TO TOUCH THE WATER'S SURFACE. FLY FISHING TAKES PATIENCE. SUDDENLY, A SILVERY RAINBOW TROUT BURSTS FROM THE WATER, CHOMPING DOWN ON THE BRIGHT YELLOW FLY ATTACHED TO THE FISHING LINE. THE BATTLE FOR ONE OF TENNESSEE'S TASTY TREASURES HAS BEGUN.

YEAR

1540 Spanish explorer Hernando de Soto arrives in Tennessee.

EVENT

Taming the Wilderness

Hundreds of years ago, Tennessee's high mountains and deep valleys were quiet places. American Indians such as the peaceful Muscogee and Yuchi people lived there. They hunted deer and buffalo and grew corn.

Then the first explorers arrived. Spaniard Hernando de Soto landed in Florida in 1539 and reached Tennessee a year later. Searching for gold but not finding any in Tennessee, he moved on. De Soto's expedition left behind diseases that killed many of the American Indians they had encountered. The land soon emptied of people.

In the 1600s, more Europeans arrived and moved into the area. The Chickasaw, Creek, and Cherokee peoples greeted French explorers. These Indian tribes were hunters and trappers, and they established trade relations with the French, including a French-Canadian fur trader named Louis Jolliet, who visited the area in 1673.

Marquette and Jolliet (opposite) traveled the Arkansas River through Tennessee about 130 years after de Soto (above) spent a month in the area.

The French set up forts from which they could trade furs with the Indians. The English arrived around the same time. France and England fought over the land in the French and

YEAR

1673   French-Canadian Louis Jolliet and Frenchman Jacques Marquette explore Tennessee.

EVENT

- 7 -

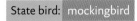
State bird: mockingbird

Indian War, which lasted from 1754 to 1763. It ended with France giving up all its land east of the Mississippi River—including Tennessee—to England.

Fur traders made many trails and trade routes in the wilderness of Tennessee, helping eastern pioneers travel west. Frontiersmen and hunters such as Daniel Boone guided settlers across Tennessee to build homes and farms. The first permanent resident of Tennessee was a man named William Bean. In 1769, he built a cabin at Boone's Creek in the northeastern corner of Tennessee. Two years later, James Robertson led many families to settle in the area. Robertson is called "The Father of Tennessee."

By the 1770s, the 13 American colonies wanted freedom from England. In 1775, the Revolutionary War began. People who wanted to avoid the war moved west. After the war ended in 1783, those people who had settled in Tennessee formed their own state. They called the state Franklin. Franklin lasted only four years, though, because in 1790 the new United States government made Tennessee a territory of North Carolina. Six years later, on June 1, 1796, Tennessee became the 16th American state.

White settlers living on American Indian lands felt threatened, so in 1838, President Martin Van Buren ordered the Indians to move out of Tennessee. Nearly 17,000 Cherokees

Daniel Boone led many settlers westward, becoming a heroic figure in American history in the process.

YEAR
1775   Daniel Boone blazes a trail across Tennessee, opening the land to settlement.
EVENT

- *9* -

After the Southerners were defeated in the Battle of Nashville (above), the fighting moved east of Tennessee.

were sent away. Some went to camps where they were kept under guard and could not leave. Others went to Indian Territory in present-day Oklahoma.

By the mid-1800s, America was divided over many issues, including slavery. In 1861, Tennessee joined the Southern states that wanted to separate from the rest of the U.S. and keep slavery legal. Despite this, many Tennesseans fought for the Northern, anti-slavery states in the Civil War. Numerous battles were fought in Tennessee.

After the Civil War, Tennessee was ruined. Thousands of soldiers had died. Families had been torn apart. Cities and homes had been destroyed. Farmland had been neglected. It took many years for Tennessee to recover, but the state's people were eager to rebuild. They built paper mills and furniture factories. They created ironworks. And they continued to farm corn and cotton. Cities such as Chattanooga, Nashville, and Memphis attracted new residents. By 1900, Tennessee had entered a new age of industry and progress.

Women helped the state rebuild after the Civil War by working in service industries such as laundering.

YEAR
1791   The first newspaper in Tennessee, the *Knoxville Gazette,* is established by George Roulstone.
EVENT

Meadows and Mountains

TENNESSEE IS SURROUNDED BY EIGHT OTHER STATES. TO ITS NORTH ARE KENTUCKY AND VIRGINIA. NORTH CAROLINA BORDERS ITS EAST SIDE. GEORGIA, ALABAMA, AND MISSISSIPPI LIE TO THE SOUTH. ACROSS THE MISSISSIPPI RIVER TO THE WEST ARE ARKANSAS AND MISSOURI. TENNESSEE'S LANDSCAPE HAS THREE DISTINCT

The eastern box turtle, which is commonly seen in West Tennessee woodlands, is the state's official reptile.

areas called Grand Divisions. They are named East, Middle, and West Tennessee.

West Tennessee lies between the Mississippi River to the west and the Tennessee River to the east. Most of Tennessee's farms are located there, where the soil is rich. Farmers grow soybeans, corn, cotton, and a grain called sorghum in their fields. Crops such as tobacco and wheat are grown in the state, too.

West and East Tennessee lie partly in an earthquake zone. The strongest earthquakes in Tennessee happened in 1811 and 1812. They created a lake that still exists. It is called Reelfoot Lake and is the only natural lake in the state. Other lakes were created by dams on rivers. Reelfoot is home to thousands of turtles. Tennessee is known as the "Turtle Capital of the World."

Middle Tennessee includes the Nashville Basin. This is a low-lying area of pastures and streams. The Nashville Basin has a high ridge all around it called the Highland Rim. Some of the land is rocky. Because people wanted a horse that would not stumble on this rough ground, the sure-footed Tennessee Walking Horse was first bred there in the 1880s.

Many Tennessee farmers still produce tobacco using traditional methods of hanging and drying the leaves.

On the southern edge of Middle Tennessee is the Sewanee Natural Bridge. This sandstone arch has a span of 50 feet (15 m) and looks like a man-made bridge. Savage Gulf, in central Tennessee, features unusual rock formations, including the Great Stone Door, a 150-foot-deep (46 m) crevice.

The Cumberland Plateau and part of the Tennessee River divide Middle Tennessee from East Tennessee. The river flows from Knoxville southwest to Chattanooga. The plateau is a high, flat land covered with dense forests.

The Great Smoky Mountains, which are part of the Appalachian Mountains, cut though East Tennessee. The Smokies, as the mountains are called, get their name from the dusty

1862   The Battle of Shiloh, one of many Civil War conflicts fought in Tennessee, rages for two days.

With 10 million visitors a year, Great Smoky Mountains National Park is America's most popular national park.

fog that hangs in the air above the treetops. Wildflowers cover the hillsides. Birdwatchers may see small, green vireos, yellow warblers, and black and red towhees flying through the trees. Adventurers may also encounter wild turkeys, raccoons, and black bears.

Hikers in the Smokies enjoy walking the Appalachian Trail near Tennessee's eastern border. The highest point in Tennessee is also the highest point on the Appalachian Trail, which runs from Maine to Georgia: Clingmans Dome stands 6,643 feet (2,025 m) high. Only half of this mountain is in Tennessee. The other half is in North Carolina.

Clouds above the Smokies collect moisture and send it down into the foothills, where people raise livestock and grow crops. Beef cattle wander through green pastures. Dairy farms dot the landscape. East Tennessee is also rich in resources such as the metal zinc and germanium, a mineral used in making computer chips. Coal and oil are other important natural resources in Tennessee.

Summers in Tennessee are hot, but winters are mild. Temperatures usually hover around an average low of 30 °F (-1 °C) in the winter. Precipitation is light on average, with three to seven inches (8–18 cm) of rain falling each month in the summer and the same amount of snow in the winter months.

More than 1,500 of the estimated 800,000 black bears in North America live in Great Smoky Mountains National Park.

YEAR
1878 More than 5,000 residents of Memphis die in a yellow fever epidemic that sweeps across the South.
EVENT

Musical Traditions

MOST PEOPLE IN TENNESSEE ARE DESCENDED FROM EUROPEAN SETTLERS. ABOUT 80 PERCENT OF THE STATE'S POPULATION IS WHITE. AFRICAN AMERICANS ARE THE NEXT LARGEST GROUP. MOST AFRICAN AMERICANS LIVE IN WEST AND MIDDLE TENNESSEE. HISPANIC AND ASIAN AMERICANS MAKE UP A SMALL PART OF THE POPULATION. VERY FEW AMERICAN INDIANS REMAIN IN TENNESSEE.

About one million Tennesseans today can trace their heritage to the Scots-Irish. In the 1700s, many people in Scotland and Ireland suffered from droughts that made farming nearly impossible. Taxes were unreasonably high, and the governments often took farmers' land. Many people fled to America. The Great Smoky Mountains and the green Appalachian valleys reminded these immigrants of their homelands. They decided to stay in Tennessee.

The immigrants were mostly from poor families. But they valued family more than money. Through hard work, they bought farmsteads and grazing land in Tennessee. Then they handed down these homes to their children. Many Scots-Irish farms have remained in the same families for generations.

Early settlers in Tennessee (opposite) found perfect grazing land at the foothills of the mountains, where horses are still raised today (above).

YEAR

1900

EVENT

Famous railroad engineer Casey Jones of Tennessee dies heroically, trying to stop a train collision.

Bluegrass musician David Harrison "Uncle Dave" Macon was also known as "The Dixie Dewdrop."

Scots-Irish folk music gave birth to a type of music called Appalachian bluegrass. This style of music has a unique sound. Stringed instruments such as violins, banjos, and guitars are the main instruments. Each musician takes a turn playing the melody. The singers sing ballads, or songs that tell stories about people and places. Bluegrass inspired the growth of modern country music in Nashville.

Radio became a popular form of entertainment in the early 1920s. Many bluegrass musicians became famous by performing on the radio. In 1925, the show *Grand Ole Opry* was first broadcast. This weekly musical radio program's early stars were such people as banjo player Uncle Dave Macon and DeFord Bailey, known as "The Harmonica Wizard."

Many singers and musicians born in Tennessee did not need to travel far to find fame. The *Grand Ole Opry* made a star of Sarah Ophelia Colley of Centerville, Tennessee. She is better known as Minnie Pearl. Roy Acuff of Maynardville was another big Opry name.

YEAR

1916   In Memphis, Clarence Saunders founds the first grocery chain in America: Piggly Wiggly.

EVENT

Every week,
entertainers such as
The Osmond Family
(below) draw fans to
the Opry with bluegrass
and country music.

Singer Elvis Presley was born in Mississippi, but his family moved to Memphis when he was 13 years old, and he always considered Tennessee his home. Presley's music was new and different. People nicknamed him "The King of Rock and Roll." Presley built a beautiful mansion in Memphis. People still visit his home, called Graceland. It is now a museum.

Today, Nashville is one of America's three major cities known for music recording (the others are Los Angeles and New York). Known as "Music City, USA," Nashville has dozens of recording companies. Some, such as Capitol Records, are huge companies. But others, such as Wild Oats Records and Barking Frog Music Group, are small and offer new singers a chance to be discovered.

Legendary entertainer Elvis Presley (opposite) still influences the country singers who hope to be discovered in Nashville's music district (above).

YEAR

1933 The Tennessee Valley Authority, the largest electrical utility company in the country, is founded.

EVENT

Making steel

Music is not the only industry in Tennessee. The state is a leading manufacturer of automobiles and auto parts and is America's second-largest producer of zinc, a metal that is important in manufacturing. Tennessee is also the leading producer of ball clay. Ball clay is used to make floor and wall tile, as well as pottery.

About half of all the industrial workers in Tennessee are concentrated in the state's four major cities: Chattanooga, Knoxville, Memphis, and Nashville. Rural areas are home to the state's beef, timber, and oil industries.

In Tennessee steel mills, new steel is made from recycled steel scrap (above), and then it can be used to manufacture many things, from car parts (opposite) to construction beams to cans.

Nissan truck assembly line

1956   Clinton High School is the first public school in Tennessee to integrate black and white students.

EVENT

Terrific Tennessee

Tennessee is a land filled with natural and man-made beauty. In 1896, for the state's 100th birthday celebration, an impressive building called the Parthenon was constructed in Nashville. Made to look exactly like the ancient Greek building of the same name, this rectangular stone structure is surrounded by tall columns. A statue of the Greek

goddess Athena stands inside it. Because of the building, Nashville is known as the "Athens of the South."

Also in Nashville is the Ryman Auditorium. It was built as a church in 1892. Then it became a music hall. In 1943, the Grand Ole Opry stage show moved in. When the Opry constructed a new building in 1974, the Ryman was left empty. But in 1994, the Ryman reopened, and concerts are now held there again.

East of Nashville, the city of Knoxville was the site of the 1982 World's Fair, whose theme was "Energy Turns the World." More than 11 million people visited the fair, for which a 266-foot-tall (81 m) steel tower was built. The tower, called the Sunsphere, still stands today. Visitors can take an elevator to the top and look out over the city.

The world beneath Tennessee's land is also magnificent. The state has more than 8,500 known caves. Experienced cavers can journey through about 100 of them. Nine of the caves are open to tourists. Every year, thousands of people visit Raccoon Mountain Caverns near Chattanooga and Bell Witch Cave north of Nashville. Some people think Bell Witch Cave is haunted by a ghost.

The full-size replica of the Parthenon (opposite) and the towering Sunsphere (above) are two of Tennessee's most spectacular landmarks.

YEAR
1968   Civil rights leader Martin Luther King Jr. is killed by gunman James Earl Ray in Memphis.
EVENT

Visitors can see southern stingrays in the 618,000-gallon (2.3 million l) Gulf of Mexico exhibit at the Tennessee Aquarium.

In addition to exploring underground worlds, visitors to Tennessee can view life under the sea at the Tennessee Aquarium in Chattanooga. This is the second-largest freshwater aquarium in the world, with more than 12,000 animals of 300 different species. Jellyfish, turtles, sharks, river otters, and even penguins swim through the aquarium's various exhibits.

Along with its many attractions, Tennessee is also famous for its energy research. In 1942, the U.S. government chose the city of Oak Ridge as a base for conducting secret weapons research. This research was used in making the first atomic bombs. Today, there are still science labs and schools at Oak Ridge. The American Museum of Atomic Energy is also located there.

Energy of a different sort can be found in Nashville during football season. Every fall, thousands of cheering fans pack LP Field to cheer for the National Football League's Tennessee Titans. The Titans started out in Houston, Texas, as the

From 2000 to 2008, the Tennessee Titans won four division championships.

YEAR

1993   The Albert Gore Research Center opens in Murfreesboro, allowing visitors to learn about Tennessee history.

EVENT

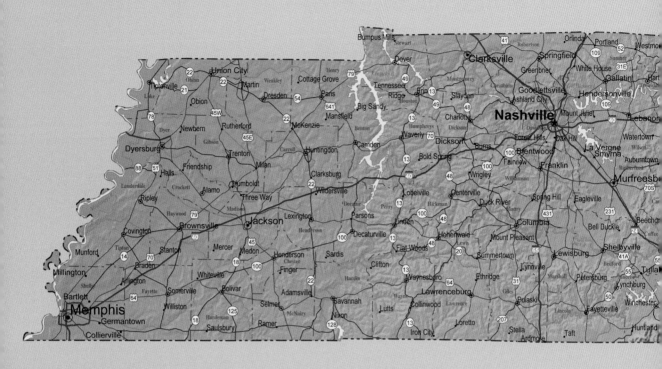

QUICK FACTS

Population: 6,156,719

Largest city: Memphis (pop. 674,028)

Capital: Nashville

Entered the union: June 1, 1796

Nickname: Volunteer State

State flower: iris

State bird: mockingbird

Size: 42,143 sq mi (109,150 sq km)—36th-biggest in U.S.

Major industries: minerals, crushed stone, timber, agriculture

Oilers. They moved to Tennessee in 1997 and got a new name two years later. The name "Titans" ties in with the image of Nashville's Parthenon, as the Titans were the first Greek gods. The team played in the Super Bowl after the 1999 season.

Tennessee's capital is also home to the Nashville Predators professional hockey team, which began play in 1998. The team logo depicts a saber-toothed cat. This logo was chosen because fossils of a saber-toothed cat were found in Nashville in 1971.

Tennessee remains a land of vast wilderness and beauty. It has inspired country music singers for nearly a century. The people of Tennessee value their traditions, but they also continue to build industries and develop cities for the next generation. West, Middle, and East Tennessee may be three Grand Divisions, but they make up one unique state that people can proudly call home.

YEAR

2006   Graceland, Elvis Presley's mansion in Memphis, is designated a National Historic Landmark.

EVENT

- 31 -

BIBLIOGRAPHY

Bergeron, Paul H. *Tennesseans and their History*. Knoxville, Tenn.: University of Tennessee Press, 1999.

Bradley, Jeff. *Moon Handbooks: Tennessee*. Emeryville, Calif.: Avalon Travel, 2005.

Lacey, Theresa Jensen. *Amazing Tennessee: Fascinating Fucts, Entertaining Tales, Bizarre Happenings, and Historical Oddities about the Volunteer State*. Nashville: Rutledge Hill Press, 2000.

State of Tennessee. "About Tennessee." Tennessee.gov. http://www.tennesseeanytime.org/about/index.html.

Tennessee Historical Society. *Tennessee History: The Land, the People, and the Culture*. Knoxville, Tenn.: University of Tennessee Press, 1998.

INDEX